The Wish

A MEMOIR OF ALL THE W

DEDICATION

To the girl
who sleeps with a heavy heart
who loved with all she could
who broke in half and yet carries on
who knows that wishes come true
who still believes in love
who dreams

This is for you.

Email: ArslanWrites@Gmail.com

Facebook: www.Facebook.com/ArslanWrites

Instagram: @ArslanWrites

Website: www.ArslanWrites.ca

Ordering Information:
Quantity sales - Special discounts are available on quantity purchases by corporations, associations, and others. For details, contact the publisher via KDP Kindle Direct Publishing.

Cover image illustrated by Syed Arslan Ali Zaidi, not to be reproduced, distributed, or transmitted in any form without prior written permission.

Interior line art illustrations used under a standard ShutterStock license. Interior handwritten art and illustrations are submitted by the loving community of Instagram artists and creatives that I wanted to give back to for their love and support. Please follow their handles and show some love.

ISBN-10: 9798650700166

First Edition

ACKNOWLEDGMENTS

This is to acknowledge everyone that believed in a third book, especially my best friend Du'a Baig for continually encouraging me and envisioning this book before the thought of it even crossed my mind. Also, anyone that is holding this book right now and proudly owns a copy - you have a special place in my heart. Thank you for your support. You are the reason I continue to write. ♡

I swear
it on all
the wishes
I've ever
made,

I haven't
wished
for anyone
as much
as you.

This is
a memoir
of all
those wishes
waiting to
come true.

Instagram: @ArslanWrites

We've been
conditioned
into believing
that love
leaves us
heartless
when it's gone;

but perhaps
the emptiness
is only an
opportunity
to start over,

and to fill
it with
the right
kind of love.

- the end is a new beginning /
emptiness is an opportunity to refill

Just
because
it runs,

it isn't
meant
for you
to chase
after.

What
is yours
will stay.

Sometimes
life goes
on while
you cease
to live,

and you
realize that
breathing
has very
little to
do with
being alive.

Not all storms are meant to destroy you. Some are sent your way to soak you enough to teach you how to swim. This too shall pass. Let this be a reminder that you have it in you to survive it.

- Just keep swimming

May
the voices
in your
head be
at peace.

May
the storms
in your
heart feel
at ease.

… and even though she had every right to feel exhausted, she carried on as if nothing had even happened.

- war child

She was not the type to be held captive. She saw freedom for what it was; a birthright.

Artist: Firdous Akrami **Instagram:** @xee_fay

In wanting to heal,
I stopped feeling.
When in fact
all I had to do was feel.
Healing begins with feeling.

Emptiness is also a part of the process of feeling whole. Often when we begin to feel numb and empty, we begin to think that this is the end. Most of the times it is. But that's only because we choose to stay there. It's like taking the bus and instead of staying on for the entire ride, you get off on the wrong stop and choose to stay there. Wherever you are right now, be it the boulevard of numbness or the avenue of emptiness, just remember you're not meant to stay there. You may have gotten off, but this was never your destination. Reroute. You have it in you get back on the bus and to make it to the next stop, and the next, and the next until you are where you're meant to be. The journey to wholeness involves collecting the pieces and gaining self awareness.

You may feel empty right now and it may last a while, but don't let it consume you. Don't let it decide for you to block out all the possibilities of feeling anything else. Don't deprive yourself of other opportunities to live, laugh and love. Sometimes a part of what we feel is also self inflicted. We punish ourselves because we begin to believe that we deserve it because we made a mistake, or we feel as if we weren't enough.

How much of your emptiness and sorrow is self inflicted? How much are your feelings of isolation are you putting yourself through what you think you deserve? I want you to take the next step and start believing in yourself again. There was a version of you before all this who knew exactly what she deserved. You knew exactly what you wanted from yourself and what you demanded from life. Although you are miles apart from feeling anything close to that, start writing those things down.

"I deserve to be happy."
"I deserve to accomplish what I want for myself."
"I can't be held back, and my past will not decide my future"
"I deserve to love and be loved, and I'll start with loving myself first."

You may not believe it at first, but believe me. I've told myself these things enough times to finally begin to believe it all. So will you.

You,
be you.

It's
the only
thing that
looks
effortlessly
beautiful
on you.

Little lady, if your struggles are larger than you and if your burdens weigh more than you can carry... and if you've held on this far and you continue to face your struggles - by now you've probably realized that even the weight of the world is nothing if you are built to withstand it. I know that time has taught you more about yourself, your inner strength and how much you can endure and overcome. You are never challenged and made to endure more than you can bear. It might seem as if it is too much but with time you will realize that if it is written for you, then surely the power to endure was also written for you before the problem itself. Stand tall, you've got this. I'm proud of who you've become and I need you to look yourself in the mirror and take pride in yourself as well. You've come a long way, and you'll get through it all the way.

I was
skeptic
at first,

but I
stopped
questioning
it the moment
our eyes
made love.

- good things do happen
to good people

One of the hardest things to do is to start over. You're not just starting over with a new person, and with a new story, and with the possibility of a whole new outcome... You're starting over with a whole new version of yourself, and it is hard because you're teaching this new version of yourself how to love and how not to love again. In fact you're learning how to love all over again because the only way you knew how wasn't enough the last time you tried. And even if you try to love the only way you know how, it is never the same love twice so you're lost and you're confused and you have no way of making sense of it. Maybe you feel things again, maybe your heart even gets excited again, but you can't process it. Your guard is up because you're on the defence, your walls are thicker than ever, and you're quick to rebuild them as soon as someone begins to get through to you. It is hard, isn't it? But you deserve another chance at love. You deserve another chance at happiness, and you deserve another chance at life. If your heart is looking for another reason to smile, give it the opportunity it deserves. It seemed like you weren't enough the last time, but perhaps you were too much for someone destined for too little. Don't deprive yourself of the chance that life is giving you. Don't be the one who regrets the chances she didn't take. I want you to try again.

- somewhere deep down there is still so much love inside of you

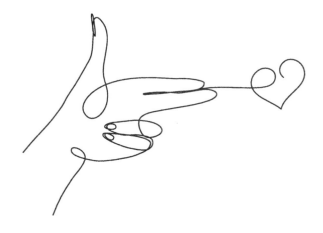

This might be the weakest you've ever been, and I will not invalidate what you feel or belittle you by saying that it's okay. It's not okay. What you feel may be heavier than anything you have ever carried in your heart before and you're allowed to feel that way. But despite the weakest you've ever been, I promise that if you hold on for a little while longer you'll realize that this is also the strongest you've ever been.

- you're a warrior

She
stood tall
against
the fiercest
of winds,

she
was a
wildflower
born out
of resilience.

Instagram: @ArslanWrites

Hope is a powerful thing.
I wish you never run out of it.

- a note to the reader

They say that in order to live a happy life, you need to lower your expectations. But when it comes to love, it's all in the expectation, isn't it? What should you expect from love? It should make you feel safe, it should make you feel like you belong. It should make you feel of value, or should make you feel better together when you're away from all the things that otherwise preoccupy your time. If all it does is fulfil your desire to touch and taste, it'll leave you empty when it has had its fill.

When you find yourself feeling like you're in love, step back and take a moment to think about exactly what you love about the person. Do they make you feel empowered? Do they make you want to try harder, and do they make you believe in yourself? Or do they leave you wondering if you're enough, and if they'd even miss you when you're not there?

Love must be emotionally fulfilling, if anything. I hope you find a love that completes you and fulfills you in a way that you have never experienced before. Anyone can touch your skin, but your soul will always be craving to be held on to. I wish that you get to experience all the beauty that love has to offer.

She's got a bit of that
sunsine in her soul;
Flowers bloom in the
hearts she touches

- ArslanWrites

Artist: Zarah Khan **Instagram:** @modamocktail

She
carried
the kind
of depth
even the
oceans
would
envy.

She
called him
an angel,

despite
the demons
inside of
him.

That's
what he
loved most
about her;

she
always
saw the
good in
people.

One day I realized that there was no such thing as the right person at the wrong time. Everything happens when its supposed to, and perhaps some things falls apart only to fall in place elsewhere. If you are consistently trying to put together something that is broken, you're probably preventing something else from falling into place. Let it be. If it needs to go, let it go.

- something great is waiting to happen

The first time I met her, I remember seeing a rainbow so up close I couldn't believe my eyes. I held her hand even tighter as we drove through the storm. That is when it hit me... Perhaps it was a sign that she was my way out of the monochromatic life I had been living all this time.

- Chromatic sense

Love is inevitable despite the inability to unlove. It is entirely possible to look to the future without fully erasing the past. How else would it teach you how to love better, and how to be loved better?

- You will love again, and there is nothing wrong with that

If my heart held me accountable for all the times I let it hurt, I would never have been able to love again. But it was forgiving when you walked into my life. Perhaps my heart knew that you had what it needed to mend again.

- another chance at love

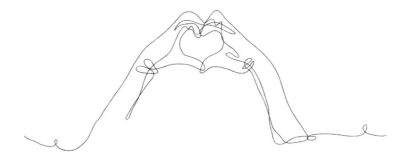

I never
realized
how lonely
I was
until I
met you.

Your
absence
taught me
what I
was missing
my entire
life.

One
of the
hardest
battles
I've ever
fought

was
fighting
the urge
to kiss
you since
the first
time I
met you.

She asked me if I've ever fallen in love.

I smiled at her thinking, "oh, I'm still falling."

- a conversation we had in my mind

Instagram: @ArslanWrites

I nearly lost my mind in trying to make the wrong one mine, until I realized that whatever is meant to be mine will not need to be convinced. It will know.

- a reminder to myself, and then you

Just as it is okay
to not be OKAY,
It is OKAY to be
Okay too!
The world doesnt
stop,
and neither should
you.

Calligraphy by: Nazia Salah **Instagram:** @nazia_salah

What
a waste
of a lifetime
it would
have been

to not
have met
you at
all

If you
ever find
yourself
looking for
the words
to define
your worth,

you are
everything
and more.

You'll notice yourself rising to the surface if you let go of all that weighs you down. If drowning you is its only purpose, it wasn't meant to be held on to in the first place.

- excess baggage

What is one thing you wish you could share with someone?

"Comfort in silence," she whispered.

Time stopped for a few moments, until their eyes met in the midst of pin drop silence.

He smiled at her, "you mean like this?"

- conversations that could have happened

Even though you gave too much of yourself to the wrong person, the little you have left to give is going to be more than enough for the right person. I hope you remember that the next time you feel you aren't enough.

- a note to the reader

One day he will come back to look for the reminiscence of his past in you, but you'll no longer be that girl. From the girl who would have left the entire world behind for him, you'll have become the girl that realized she was worth way more than who he took for granted.

Instagram: @ArslanWrites

A rush of belonging wildly ran through her veins. In that moment she knew that the feeling of longing was the absence of having never been held by love before.

- in the arms of the beloved is home

If you're looking for something beautiful on this page, you'll find what you're looking for within the person flipping through this book. This isn't a poem, but a reminder of how beautiful you are.

- I hope this made you smile

It was
a taste
of bliss,

the first
time we
kissed.

I cursed
myself for
all the chances
I missed
up until then.

Perhaps we fell in love far before we even realized, almost as if we had always been in love with one another. I can't recall the exact moment I knew it was love, almost as if I was in love with you the entire time.

Artist: Firdous Akrami **Instagram:** @xee_fay

I thought to myself whether or not it is worth a mention; a love that takes so much of you for granted and gives nothing but pain in return.

"Would poetry otherwise exist?" I chuckled beneath my breathe.

"Perhaps it wouldn't. Pain is a prerequisite to good poetry."

- pillow thoughts

"I wish I were talented like you," she complained. "I'm not good at anything."

"You're good at loving," he replied.

- what he should have said

I never understood why poets have glorified unrequited love so much so that I too was perplexed by it. It was only after it left its undying mark on me that I learned to realize that it is wrongfully glorified. There is nothing glorious about love that is never reciprocated. There is nothing glorious about being taken for granted.

- realizations

Although sometimes I wished she could find the right words, she always found a way to speak to me in a way I understood more than words could ever mean to me.

- love languages

There will be days when the voices in your head are louder than your will to silence them. Those are the days you need someone to hold on to the most. I hope you never find yourself lonely on one of those days.

- a note to the reader

At first
I didn't
know what
to do with a
love like
yours.

Prior
to you,

no one
ever loved
me the
way I wished
to be loved;

unconditionally.

I pray that whomever finds you will love you so much that when you see your reflection, you will no longer recognize the woman you've become. Far too often the aftermath of what we call "love" is a reflection of our broken self. However, a woman that is loved the way she deserves to be loved surpasses her own potential. May you become ten times the woman you want to be one day. May the man in our life be encouraging, emotionally supportive, and may he believe in you especially on the days you forget to believe in yourself.

- you are a Queen

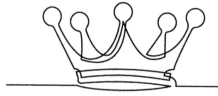

It is normal to feel skeptical. What else would you expect to feel after continually chasing someone and being taken for granted? You have gotten used to the feeling of neglect and having to prove yourself. So much so that when someone finally loves you for who you are, you find it hard to believe that it would come so easy. But love is meant to come easy. Think of it this way, the right pieces of the puzzle are meant to fit effortlessly. Only the wrong ones require a struggle, and despite all your wholehearted efforts they still won't fit. If the piece fits, then I can almost guarantee the real thing has come knocking on your door. I hope you recognize it when it comes to you; too often we fail to give the right kind of love the chance it deserves because we are too focussed on asking why we deserved to have been broken by the wrong person.

If I was drowning in water
I would have learned to swim.
If my test was to conquer heights
I would have climbed as high as I could.
If it were a trial of depths
then by God I would have fallen.
Perhaps this emptiness is just
one end of the hour glass,
and the real test is an uncertainty
of time which I must learn to endure.

- trials and tribulations

Like water
the wrong
ones will
try to
contain you

but you'll
slip right
between
their fingers.

Until one day,
you'll find
the one
who will
realize

that you
make up
most of
what they
are.

- like water

You
deserve
someone
who doesn't
just ignore
the weird
in you,

but
acknowledges
you for being
their type of
weird.

- weirdo ♡

She struggled with words, But her eyes spoke volumes.

Calligraphy by: Nazia Salah **Instagram:** @nazia_salah

If there
is such
a thing
as another
life,

I hope
you're
meant for
me again

and I
can find
you far
earlier than
I did
this time.

- lost time

You will find the right person, but you won't always have things in common. You will soon realize that even though your spirit is effortlessly attracted to one another, you still have differences. Your partner might be into swords, long drives, photography and things you will have no clue about while you might enjoy reading and long walks on the beach. You will also need to learn to connect emotionally, and intellectually to grow together. Both of you will need to try and step outside of your comfort zones and learn what the other loves. At times it will feel like fire and water, and when you refuse to understand each other to connect beyond desire, water will eventually put the fire out. You will need to accept that the two of you will always be fire and water, and that may never change. But remember it is the fire from the sun and the water from the skies that makes the earth grow. Let your love be like the soil, and take in what you can from one another. Love will grow.

- fire and water

If she
craves the
company
of your
soul before
she craves
you between
her legs,

you will
have touched
her in a
way no one
could ever
fulfill her
the same.

I often
find myself
lost in
thoughts,

of my
lips tangled
in yours
like knots.

I can
taste you,

in everything
I love.

The Wishing Flower

Make a Wish.

I wish for yours to come true for you.

I dodged
you like
a bullet,

in the end
it was you
that showed
me how to live.

A part
of me
died when
my beloved
left.

It was
only after
I met you
that I
realized why
what was left
of me fought
so hard to
survive.

at times
I wish to go
so far away,
that even I can
no longer find myself.

Artist: Firdous Akrami **Instagram:** @xee_fay

There will be times when she will wonder how you put up with her. She will wonder how you don't get bored of her stories when she tells you about the parts of her day that she will question having wasted your time with later. She will question why you chose to be with her, and why you are willing to stay. You might tell her this often, or perhaps you might not tell her often enough. But that's when she needs you to tell her that you love her, that's when she'll need to hear it the most.

- confirmation

You
believed
in the
version of
me

that
I stopped
trying to
become.

This
is a
thank you
for not giving
up on me

even though
I had given
up on
myself.

Together
we have
never
spent a
moment
alone.

Love
was always
between
us.

She wished to be loved softly
and I had the love of wild in me.
When we came together,
I awoke her beast while
she calmed the savage inside of me.

All the wars I've lost have taught me one thing; in the battlefield of love it is who you love most that ultimately decides your fate. In order for you to love me, I must love myself most. Only then can I teach you how to love, and only then will the war of love be fair.

If you
are ever
made to
feel like
an option,

choose
yourself.

I was
born with
storms
in me,

that
stood still
at the
thought
of you.

I'm still trying to figure out whether you walked out of one of my dreams, or if I'm living inside of one. It scares me to think that I might wake up from whatever this is as soon as I begin to think all of it is real.

Instagram: @ArslanWrites

I don't
know at
what point
in time
it will
happen,

but
it will.

You
will heal,

and that
I promise.

- a note to the reader

She took
offence to
sympathy.

She
wasn't
a victim,

but a warrior.

Whatever
broke you
is gone.

Sometimes
you need
to realize
that it
only hurts

because
you are
still holding
on.

- let go

Though her touch was soft,
She had this very command and conquer
kind of thing about her.

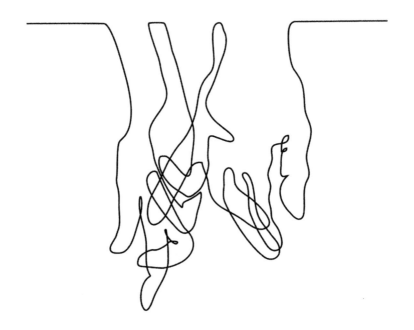

You be you.
It's the only thing
that look
EFFORTLESSLY
Beautiful
on you.

Calligraphy by: Nazia Salah **Instagram:** @nazia_salah

Instagram: @ArslanWrites

One day you'll realize that strength has very little to do with muscle. Strength is an attitude. Not the kind of attitude where you're narcissistic and disrespectful, but the kind where you're headstrong and know you can conquer anything that comes your way.

You can be as soft as a feather and as kind as ever but still be ruthless in your pursuit of whatever you want for yourself.

So this is to appreciate the strength of a woman, who is in many ways stronger than a man - in the way she endures, and in the way she stands up for herself despite the challenges that come her way.

True strength isn't all muscle, it's also willpower and endurance. Little lady, this is for the fight inside of you.

- more power to you ♡

Sometimes we deliberately play games when there is absolutely no room for them. Sometimes we ruin something so beautiful in trying to prove a point to ourselves, or we are seeking validation, or trying not to look desperate, or even overthinking what requires no thought at all. The sexiest thing you can do is just be yourself, without any thought involved and stay true to who you are. Desperate or not, who cares what it seems like? If love is being reciprocated, then do your part and give it all you've got to hold on to it and make it last.

It's the unnecessary games that ruin perfectly beautiful things, such as what deliberately waiting between texting back can do that even being kilometres apart couldn't have done otherwise.

- games can validate distance

At times
the sound
of approaching
footsteps was
my own
heartbeat in
the anticipation
of you.

Your heart was never meant to be domesticated and given boundaries to dream and grow within. Your voice was never meant to be silenced and your dreams of possibilities were never meant to be defined for you. Do you remember the time when there were no barriers to what you thought possible, and no extents to which you thought you could go? Perhaps you've come so far ahead and left the thought of it all so far behind. Perhaps you stopped dreaming and woke up to fulfill someone else's dream, and reality became an illusion of what is meant to be. But there is a fire in you that is only aroused by a certain kind of wind. There is a wild horse inside you that only craves a certain type of freedom. There is a purpose in you that you have somehow learned to suppress, a will in you that you were told to forego. But that is what you were made for. That is who you are, but you were taught to let it go and chase after what everyone else thought was right.

Somewhere along the way you learned that you do not decide for yourself and your wilderness was domesticated. You did not grow, but you existed long enough to convince yourself of growth. But what I wish for you is for the right winds to arouse your fire again so you burn lustfully with purpose. I wish for your wilderness to be free so your heart runs like a wild horse and doesn't just beat to assist you in merely existing. I pray for you to silence all that you hear and let your inner voice scream to you that it wishes to unlearn all that it has been taught, and I wish that you find it in you to listen to the inner voice and take control of your purpose.

You were sent here for a reason, with a certain something that no-one else has. Perhaps your voice was to be heard and not meant to become an echo. Perhaps your pen was supposed to write scripts and not just scribbles. Perhaps you were meant to be a light but you were taught to settle for being dim.

I want to remind you that your dream is yours to fulfil, not to be archived. You only have one life to do it. Your wilderness is meant to be free and not be tamed. You are your own person. Unlearn all that you were taught about yourself, and embrace yourself for who you always knew you were. Wild and free, entitled to your own idea of growth.

There will be days when you'll have so much to say,
and then there will be days when no amount of words
will be enough to express what you feel.

- you can choose to remain silent

I'm sorry if the silence scares me at times, and I'm sorry if it seems like I rush to cut some conversations shorter than others. You're allowed to have days where you'll have nothing to say, and you'll want to hear me instead. The only thing I'm afraid of is not being able to say enough on those days for you to realize that perhaps I might not be enough at all.

- insecurities

One afternoon I noticed that the scorching summer sun had barely burnt me. Thats when the thought had first occurred to me. Lovers resonate so well with tinted window as they too shade you until they break. They burn for you to be at ease. As strange as it sounds, we have all been a tinted window to someone. I hope you've never had to break.

The thing with broken windows is that the shards have the potential of hurting other people. It's strange if you think about it, how broken people often hurt those who are not at fault. I hope you care for your sharp edges if it ever comes to that. I also hope you have someone to shade you on those hot summer days as well.

- tinted window

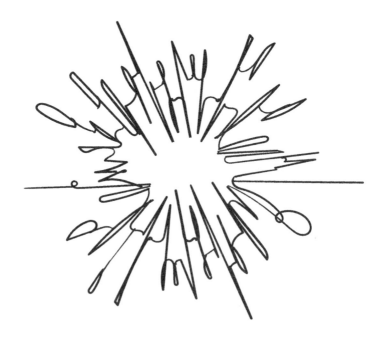

Love
could be
terribly tragic,

and
still feel
like magic.

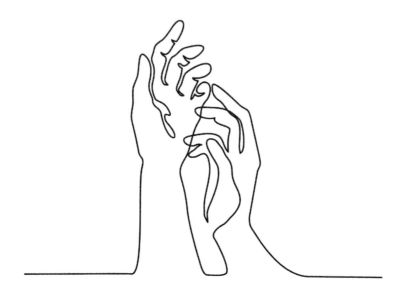

There
was a
howl in
her soul
that yearned
for the moon.

She
had the
heart of a wolf,

and
she in
herself
was a pack
of her own.

- she wolf

At some point in your life, you are left to fend for yourself. You might realize that you're on your own and any attachments that you have may not be loyal, the people that surround you may not understand you, and may be toxic to your growth. You'll have people wanting to make choices for you, signifying your obedience with their honour, or manipulating you into forgoing your own will. You might feel lonely, but just as there is weakness in loneliness… there is also inner strength that can be uncovered through loneliness. There is comfort in numbers and satisfaction in belonging, but there will be times when not everyone will be on the same page as you. There will be times when you must stand up for yourself. Your soul is a traveller, and each soul is destined to partake in a journey of its own. If there are storms within you that can not be controlled; if there is a wild in you that refuses to be tamed, then that is who you are. There is a purpose to your existence far greater than you can imagine, and there are yearnings your heart can not ignore.

Maybe it is love, maybe it is education, maybe it is a longing for some destination. Embrace what your yearning calls out to. Maybe you're not meant to follow, but are made to lead. Some come from tribes, some help build them, but some carry a tribe within them. Perhaps you are your own tribe. There are some battles you need to fight on your own, and there are some choices you need to make for yourself.

Today I won't tell you what you've been programmed into wanting to hear; that you're as beautiful as a rose, and as delicate. I won't tell you that there is strength in your thorns. I won't tell you that you'll bloom, and blossom. Life isn't all rainbows and butterflies, its also standing your ground and carrying scars. Today I want to remind you of what you haven't yet been told, because you just might grow the strength and fight for yourself. Today I want to remind you of how fierce you are. Dear she-wolf, you are in yourself a pack of your own.

Unlearn all that you
were taught about
yourself,
and embrace you for who
you always knew you were,
Wild & Free,
entitled to your own
idea of
Growth.

Calligraphy by: Nazia Salah **Instagram:** @nazia_salah

She
carried
softness
like a sword.

Her
smile would
slay demons.

She's
got a bit
of that
sunshine
in her
soul,

flowers
bloom
in the
hearts she
touches.

She
gave herself
a thousand
excuses not
to love,

and
yet she
did.

He
alone was
reason enough
to defy a
thousand
objections of
her own.

This is for the over-thinker... She's given herself a thousand excuses not to love you, to save herself, and to avoid any attachment. She's thought of it all, not once, not twice... But over and over again, night after night. If she's finally given in, it means that she's given herself reason after reason to why she'd risk her heart again.

It's nice having her attention because she doesn't compromise in how much of herself she gives you, she gives it her all. It is also very easy taking her for granted, because who doesn't mind being the centre of someone's entire world? But don't let your sense of entitlement make you break her heart. Be careful, especially if you have no intention of making things work.

Don't grab her attention, engage her curiosity, and take her for a wild ride into a world of dreams where she plans every little detail out only for you to tell her that she deserves better, because trust me... She already thought of that and she still convinced herself over and over again that it is you she wants to make things work with.

- nothing hurts more than building an entire life of your dreams around lies

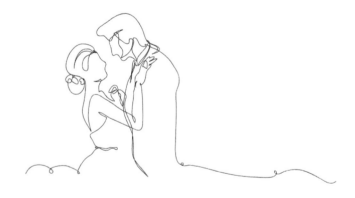

"I'm
not like
the rest
of them,"

she insisted
from time
to time;

As if
it wasn't
enough for
him to tell,

that his
inclination
towards her
was divine.

She
is a little
bit of a
legend,

and
she doesn't
even know it.

"You fight like a girl," should not
bruise little egos but validate
strength and resilience.

One day I will teach my son that
strength is not only being able to
lift heavier, but also to carry on
when your heart feels the heaviest.

- dedicated to my sister

Her:
"One day
I want you
to experience
all the colours
of the world."

Him:
"I have
experienced you.
You are colour."

- colourblind

I was
always
content
with being
half full,

until your
absence
became a
reminder
of how
empty
I was
without
you.

"What
keeps you
up at night?" He asked.

"Nothing
in particular,
really.

Just
everything
all at once," she whispered.

She struggled with words,
but her eyes spoke volumes.

When someone speaks your language, you won't have to worry about finding the right words. Communication becomes effortless, it just flows. And I don't mean your local dialect, or the national language, or your secret emoji code. Your soul has a language very few dare to understand, and that's the language of the eyes. It is the language of silence, it is in the actions of a person. You can speak through the way you look at someone. It's much deeper and more meaningful than the language of words.

At the end of the day, words are just words. They're empty. They deceive, they're open to interpretation, and misinterpretation. They warrant overthinking, they are sometimes not enough, and sometimes don't even hold the right meaning. But there is a deeper understanding that goes beyond what words could ever convey. It goes beyond emojis, beyond text messages and phone calls. Not everyone will speak your love language, but when you find the few who do - you'll never have to explain. Not having to explain yourself is a luxury between two people.

You can use all the words in the world, and sometimes a person will never understand despite the effort you put into explaining. With the language of your soul, you won't have to utter a word and your person will know.

I hope whomever finds you speaks your language. You say so much, and sometimes nothing at all - but there's a depth in your eyes that demands to be understood. Sometimes your words say one thing, and your eyes say another.

- I pray it never goes unnoticed

Before you respond, step back and pause for a moment. How you respond will either validate or invalidate her insecurity. Sometimes love requires patience, and a little bit of it goes a long way. The only way to make her believe she has nothing to worry about is to react appropriately. Sometimes playing defence is the same as being on the offensive. Remember, you're on the same team.

- you both need to win

All a good woman really wants is for you to be with her and love her in return for all the love she showers you with. All she expects is effort and attention. You don't have to go chase wealth to keep her, in fact, all you really need is to appreciate her. When you find her, you'll realize how simple she really is. She'll find happiness in the smallest of things. Walks in the park will feel like vacations to her as long as she has your attention. A single rose, and unexpected phone calls, surprise visits in between lunch breaks at work, or window shopping at the mall. That's all it really takes to make her happy. But you need to be careful, because she'll sense it as soon as you pull back. She is very detail oriented, and she'll notice the smallest changes in your behaviour. She'll know and it'll break her knowing that you are no longer making efforts to keep her. When you find a good woman, don't awaken her love for you only so you could leave her. There are far too many good women out there who gave up on love because a man chose to lead her on only to deceive her.

You will look at me with confusion because you wish to see a misguided version of what a man should be. I am not as man as you, but more. My voice is deeper than the roars of thunder, for if it were man it would sound like me. My eyes show no mercy like a beast in the wild, for if it were man it would glare like me. My anger is that of a calamity at which you'd tremble, for if it were man it would unleash like me. My pride is more lethal than that which would make you fall to your knees, for if it were man it would be as unjust as me. My desires are more lustful than that of the devil himself, for if it were man it would seduce like me. My hate is more vengeful than that of any force of nature, for if it were man it would obliterate like me. With all my power, and all my might... I am only but a man. What gives me the right to oppress a woman? I have met with the fragility of a woman, and felt it to be as vulnerable as my ego, for if it were man it would break like me... I have fought alongside the strength of a woman and experienced her wrath, for if it were man it would be as indestructible as me. I have fallen in love with the mercies of a woman and have been healed by her compassion, for if it were man it would be as gentle as me. I have seen her to be as equal in strength to me, and possibly even stronger. I have learned she is as limitless as me, and possibly even more over achieving. I have known her to be as brave as me and possibly even more courageous. She is everything I am, and everything I can never be. Therefore the man in me can not own her or treat her like property. I am her guardian, and she is mine to watch over me. That is what logic has taught me of what a man is, and what man should aim to be. For if logic were man, it would preach like me.

- manhood

At
times
I wanted
nothing more
than to be held.

All
my might
crumbled
at the sight
of you.

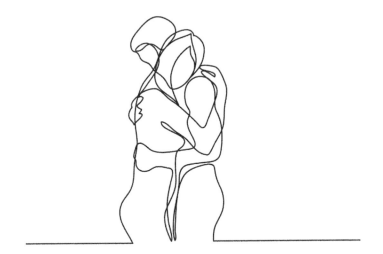

Rise and shine. No really - get out of bed and show the world what you are made of. The universe did not come together one night in creating you, only to find you hopelessly hiding away in the dark one day. You are a beacon of hope; a shining light that is so much more than the sun, the moon, and all the stars combined. Your smile alone can outshine it all. Whatever it is that is holding you down is not worth the dimming of your soul. You'll find a way to get through it, but until you do… Rise and shine, beautiful.

Though her touch was
soft
She had this very
Command & Conquer
kind of thing about
Her

Calligraphy by: Nazia Salah **Instagram:** @nazia_salah

If it
so happens
that you
love again,

I hope
I at least
taught you
how to be
loved.

She
was not
the type
to be held
captive.

She saw
freedom
for what
it was;

a birthright.

  - breaker of chains

It was on one evening in June of 2020 when we met for a quick catch up. It had been months since I last met this friend. He had been through a lot during this time without speaking a word or letting me know. He asked how I had been, and reluctantly I spoke without giving it much thought. He caught me mid sentence without an ounce of hope and he cut me off. I don't know how he did it, but I guess when you have been down rough paths you become familiar with those who have traveled down similar roads. He said these beautiful words:

"You are the kind of person, I would come to for advice. You have always been that, and I know that people come to you when they are down and you give them hope. They come to you for advice right?"

I shook my head in agreement.

"Be that person to yourself. Take your own advice."

For a few moments I was caught off guard, and I couldn't help but burst out in a somewhat nervous laughter. Why is it that we forget to give ourselves advice on our darkest days, but we are so quick to unravel and care for the minds of others? Is it that we don't believe what we tell them, or don't find ourselves worthy enough at some point to even take our own advice?

I thought about this for a while, and I realized - somewhere along the way I had begun to belittle myself. It needed to stop, and all I needed was to be reminded of who I was.

I am sure you are also the kind and caring soul that people turn to when they are in need, and I am sure that you jump at the first opportunity to make sure they are okay and you give them the best possible advice to save them from themselves.

It's time we also saved ourselves.

- for Harpreet

It's
in the
way those
words roll
off of your
tongue,

as if
we're in
the midst of
making love.

I can
always tell
you mean it
when you
say it,

because
it has never
sounded so
good.

- "I love you."

I sat
beneath the
milky way,

staring up
at all its
glory with
nothing but the
thought of you
in mind.

Those were
the only two
things that could
take my breathe away:

you and a sky
full of stars.

- Tobermory

Instagram: @ArslanWrites

She spoke her mind with him
including things she never
imagined herself saying out loud.
From her dreams to her wildest fantasies,
every layer of her exposed.
Perhaps true love was naked in itself,
and taking off your clothes had
nothing to do with it.

- naked

When you share your past with him and you find that your voice shakes with hesitance, is it because you expect him to forgive you for it? Please remember that your past is yours to forgive. Forgive yourself of the past or you will hold on to it and stay stuck in the negative patterns of blaming yourself for it. Accept it for what it is, it is over. Do this so you don't find yourself ashamed of it and providing explanations in expectations of forgiveness. Instead, you will find yourself showing gratitude for allowing the past in doing everything it could to help you embrace a version of yourself committed to growth. There is no shame in growing, and there is no apologizing for what led to your growth.

- growing with grace

I have experienced how it feels to be drowning in negativity, and it got to a point where the negativity became so toxic to my well being that I couldn't deal with it anymore. I was at a point where I began talking to myself while imagining scenarios in my head and having arguments with all the toxic people in my life. I was planning these conversations thinking of all the possible hurtful comebacks that I could think of, and I had no regret about the vile things that I thought of saying. But these were either conversations that never happened, or when they happened I was too tired from all the battles I fought within myself that I had no energy left in me to say those things aloud.

When I finally had enough, I reflected on the fact that all this negative energy was doing is draining me. It was changing me. It made me into such a bitter person filled with so much venom that I began to realize perhaps this is what the toxic people in my life are dealing with as well and I happen to be on the receiving end of the energy they are releasing. I was becoming like the very people that I was up against, and I didn't want that for myself. If I didn't do anything about it, perhaps one day someone else would have found themselves on the receiving end of my negative energy for doing nothing to deserve it but having loved me.

The only solution was space. I loved them and they loved me, but neither of us realized what their unhappiness was doing to me. I distanced myself from their energy so my own energy could thrive within me.

So if you need to take a few steps back for yourself, there is absolutely nothing wrong with that. Your heart is far too precious to turn cold because of the energy around you. Your mind is far too beautiful to be clouded with negativity.

Your vibe makes the world a better place. Take care of yourself.

She
loved with
the kind
of love

that would
make you
believe in
love again.

Her
vibe was
irreplaceable,

she
had the
kind of soul
that would
make even
the broken
hearted
whole
again.

Instagram: @ArslanWrites

Take all the time you need.
Healing does not come with deadlines,
nor do you owe your healing to anyone.

Far too many women are taught to compromise and accept the kind of half-hearted love they receive from people who don't know how to love. Be the kind of woman who knows where the exit is when your love doesn't receive the hospitality it deserves.

- love should not ask you to compromise your self respect

I named a star after us,
so that even if we were
to die without having been one…

Our love would still
burn in the heavens above.
Perhaps one day,
lovers will wish upon our star.

- Leo Minor 11393647

Such a day will come when
you will wake up and
your heart will feel much lighter.
I wish you keep on loving
the way you have always loved.
I wish you heal from what broke you,
and your strength becomes hope for those around you.
I wish that you never stop making wishes.
I wish that you never stop believing in miracles.
I wish that you never stop dreaming.

- goodbye, precious.